Heidi & Daniel Howarth

What Makes Me Brave?

Sky Pony Press
New York

2

All around there is the sound of scratching.
The sound of tiny flippers moving against the warm golden sand.
The sound of new lives beginning.

So Little Turtle wiggles and Little Turtle pushes and his soft egg splits and the sand parts.
He knows deep inside that now is the time he needs to be brave.

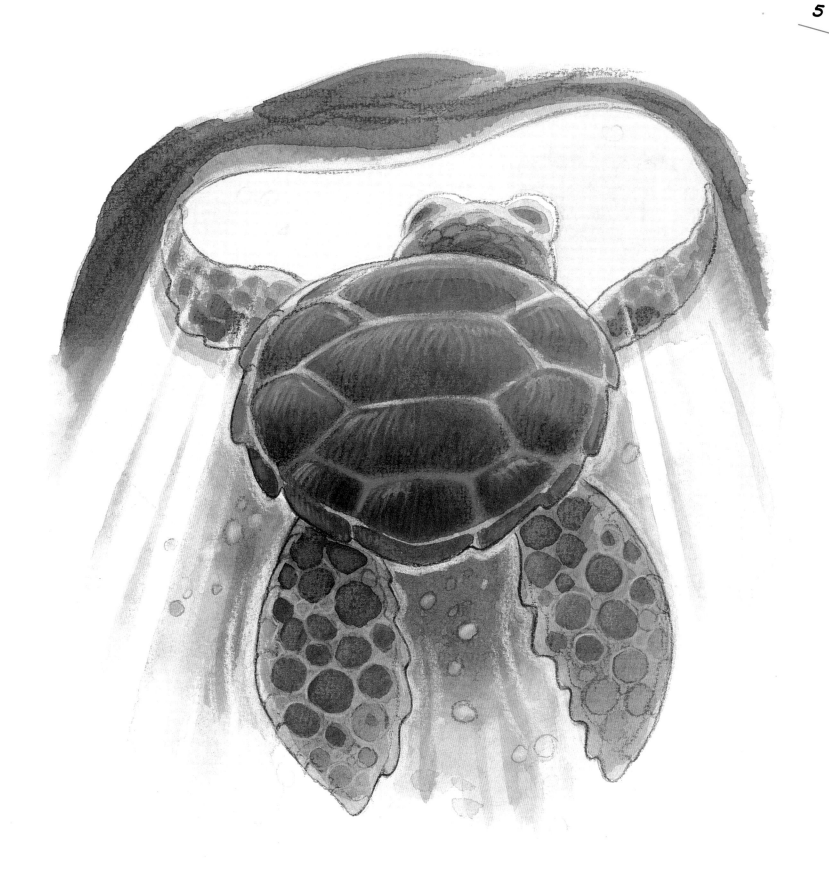

He rushes across the sand. It is warm and dry under
his soft belly and his flippers push hard to move him along.
All around him, other turtles are rushing too. They have
to be brave, they have to be quick, and they have to be fast.

Instinct is all they have; no mommies
or daddies are there to help them.
Little Turtle can see the sea, smell the salt
and the safety.

He pushes hard, as brave
and as fast as his little
flippers can carry him.
He does not look up;
he is focused on the ocean.
He has to get there fast.
Above him there is danger;
the seagulls call.

As a wave crashes down on him, he feels the cold water
for the first time.
He must be brave; he must swim. He takes a big deep breath
and he is under.
He must swim, swim as hard as he can, to the safety
of the deeper water.

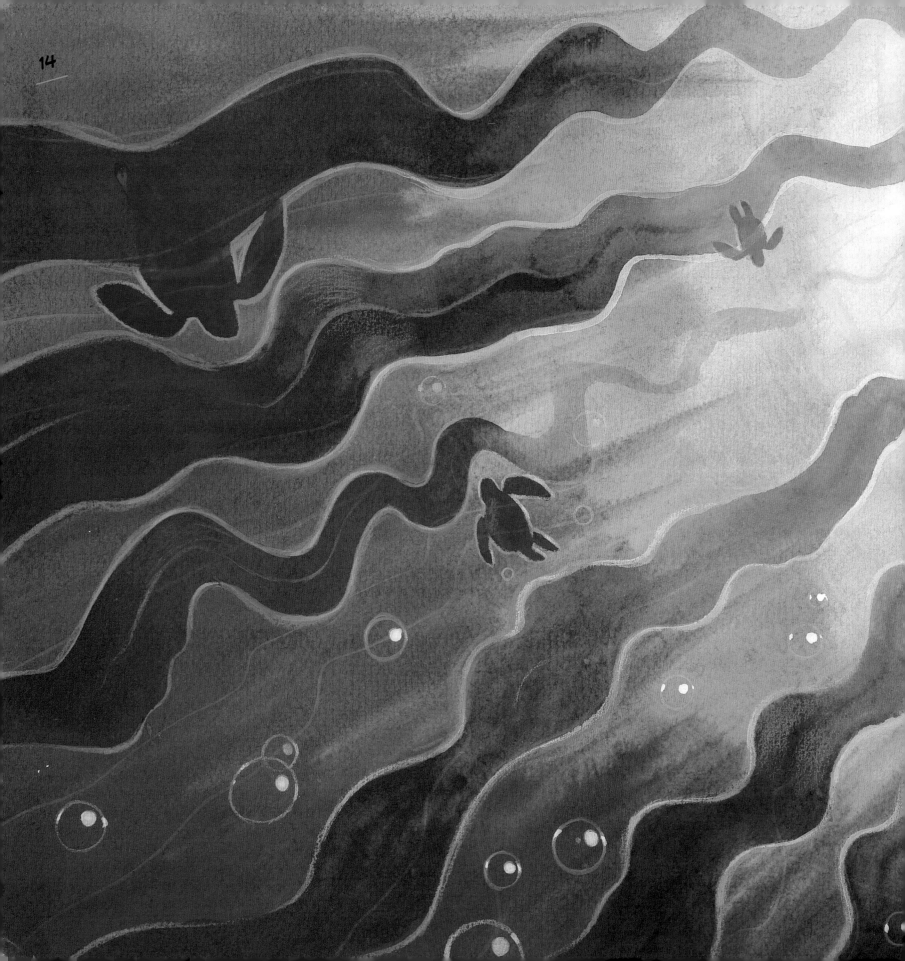

The water is warm and calm here and he needs to rest.
He stops in the seaweed, in the calm of
the shallows and in the safety of the reef.
Dark shadows sometimes cross overhead
and all the little turtles swim and hide
in the safety of the long ribbons of kelp.

He is not the only one hiding
here. He is worried, but curious
too, so he swims deeper
into the green weeds.
"Hello," says a little voice.
"Hi there," calls another.

As the bright sun shines through the water, soon he can see that he was not the only brave turtle on the beach. Many other bright little eyes are looking at him too.

Their soft green shells blend in well.
They are hidden, camouflaged.

Here it is safe to play, safe to eat, and safe to grow.

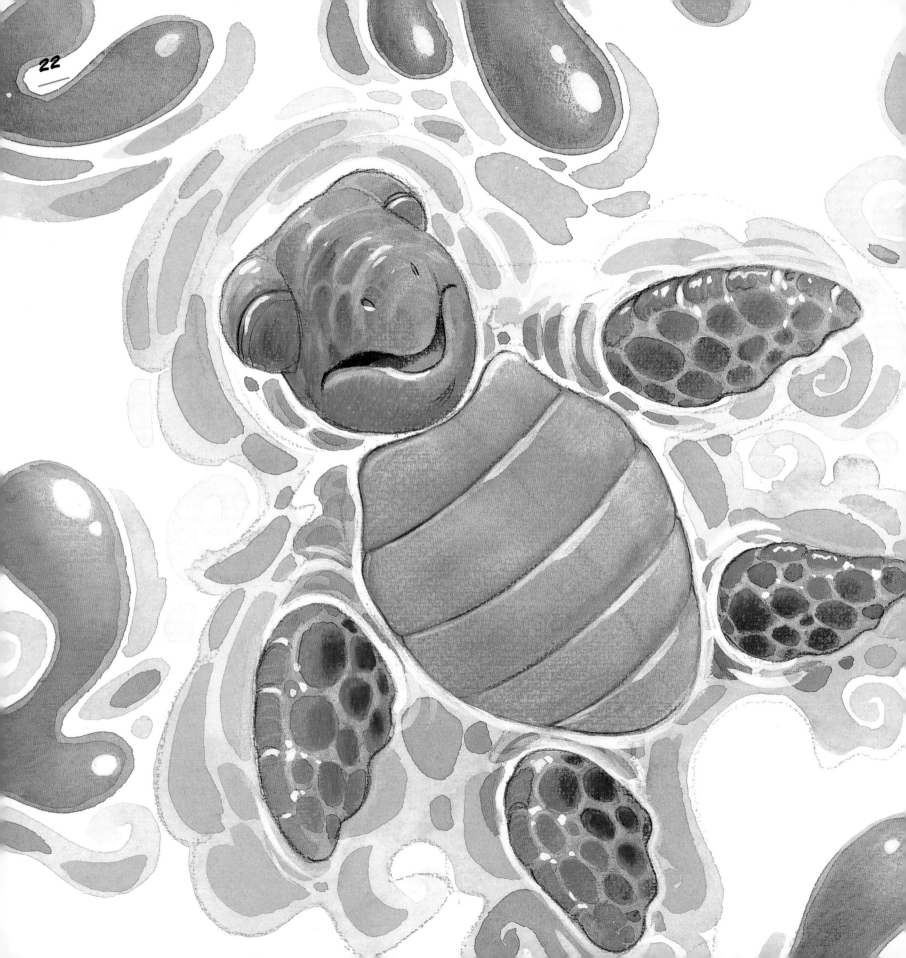

On bright sunny days, they sometimes swim
to the surface and let the nice golden sun warm
their soft shells that are now beginning to harden.
Time moves by and the turtles grow. They swim
many miles, exploring the vast ocean and seeing many
beautiful creatures along the way.

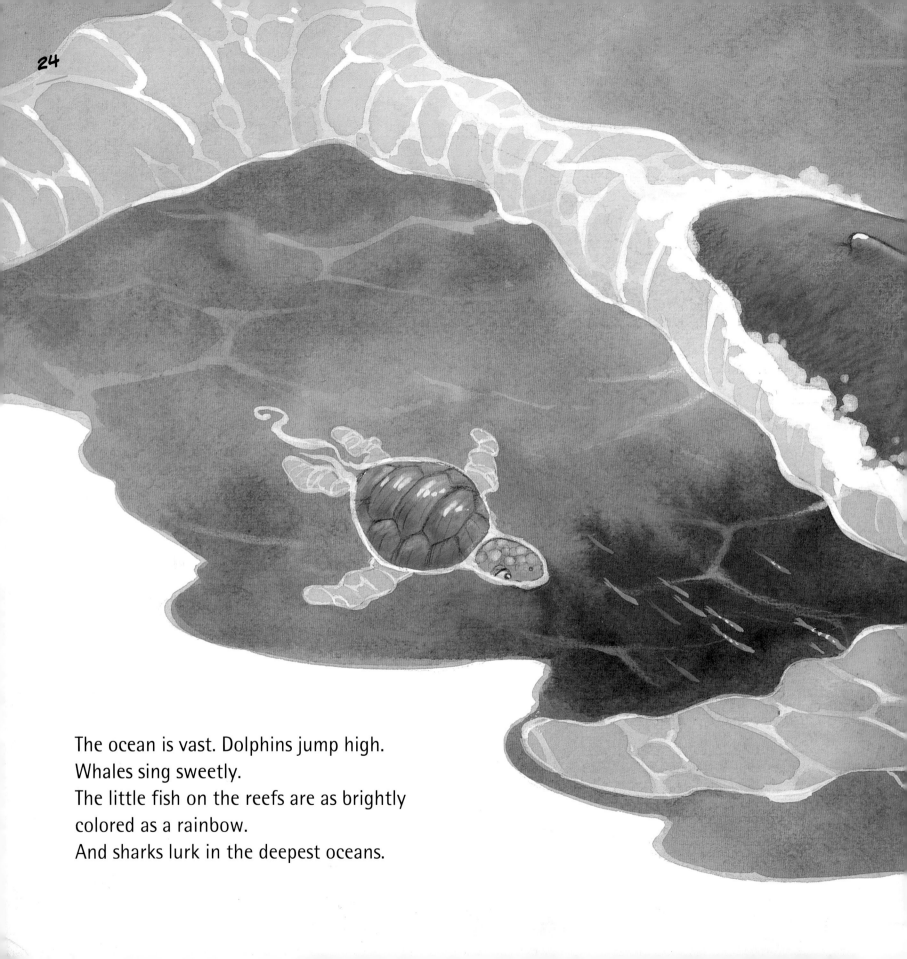

The ocean is vast. Dolphins jump high.
Whales sing sweetly.
The little fish on the reefs are as brightly
colored as a rainbow.
And sharks lurk in the deepest oceans.

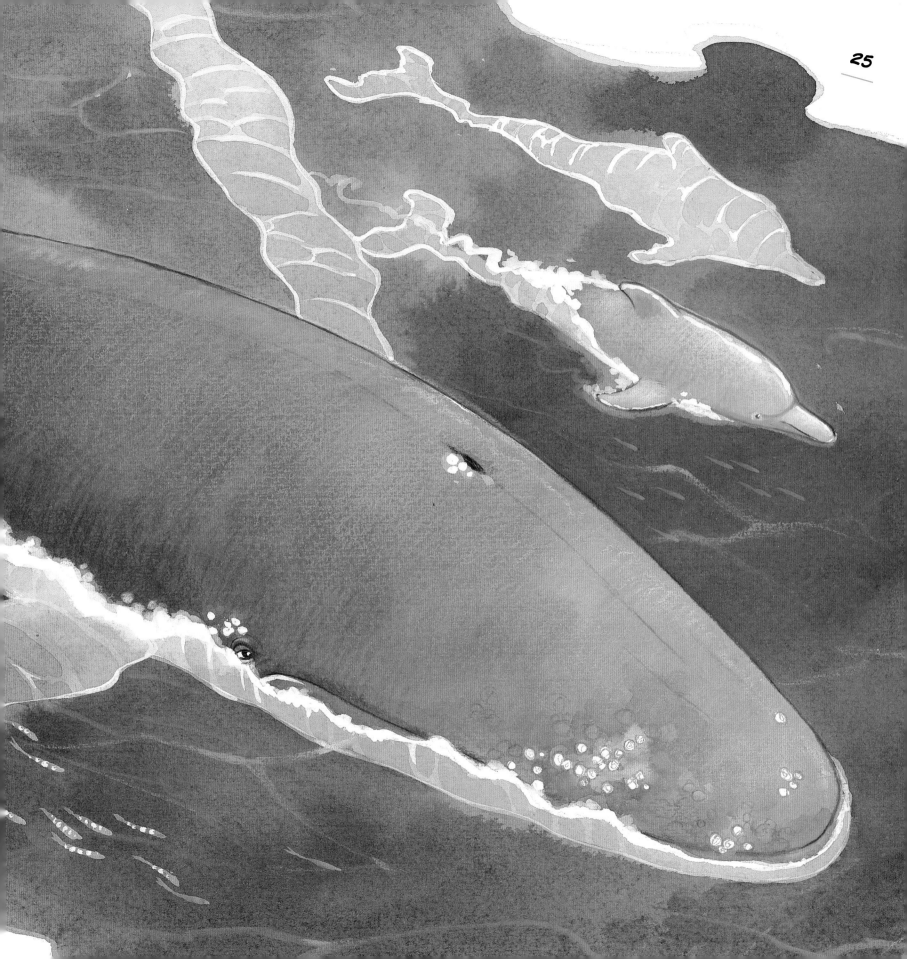

Little Turtle is happy
as he swims all alone.
When he is fully grown
he will return to his home.

He will find the place where he hatched, where
his bravery began.
He will find a wife and this life cycle can begin again.

He lives in the ocean.
He will be here for a hundred
years or more.
Nothing really scares him,
not any more.

He is very old now with barnacles on his shell.
A cheeky anemone that clings there as well.
He swims in the current. He plays in the surf.
He no longer needs to feel brave.
He smiles at the little ones playing nearby.
He knows their lives will be long and
wonderful too.

What **makes** me feel **brave**

Many animals have wonderful and interesting life cycles.
The turtle is no exception.
To start with, a mummy turtle lays some eggs.
She buries them in warm sand and leaves them to grow.
They take two months to grow and then they hatch.

Ask the children about other animals
that lay eggs.
Is it just birds?
Well a turtle is not a bird, is it?

Turtles have been around in our oceans for 230 million years.

They were here before some other very famous egg-layers that are now extinct: The dinosaurs. Did the children know that dinosaurs laid eggs?

The dinosaurs are extinct. Do the children know what that word means?
The dinosaurs died after a comet hit the Earth and altered the planet, but many animals have become extinct because of things people have done.

This is a dodo. It was a big friendly flightless bird. It was hunted and eaten by humans until there were none left.

Some turtles are now very rare.
They can get caught in fishing nets and because they breathe air, they can drown!
Their favorite food is jellyfish. But this is also a problem for them. Many turtles die every year from swallowing plastic carrier bags (the ones you put your shopping in at the supermarket), mistaking them for jellyfish.

But humans are now helping the turtle. There are special beaches where their eggs are now protected. So hopefully they will be around for another 230 million years.

What Makes Me Brave?

Sky Pony Press books may be purchased in bulk at special discounts for sales promotion, corporate gifts, fund-raising, or educational purposes. Special editions can also be created to specifications. For details, contact the Special Sales Department, Racehorse for Young Readers, 307 West 36th Street, 11th Floor, New York, NY 10018 or info@skyhorsepublishing.com.

Sky Pony® is a registered trademark of Skyhorse Publishing, Inc.®, a Delaware corporation.

Visit our website at www.skyhorsepublishing.com.

10 9 8 7 6 5 4 3 2 1

Author: Heidi Howarth
Illustrations: Daniel Howarth
Design and layout: Gemser Publications, S.L.
Cover design: Mona Lin

Library of Congress Cataloging-in-Publication Data is available on file.

Print ISBN: 978-1-5107-4552-0
Ebook ISBN: 978-1-5107-4566-7

Printed in China